Creating
Early America␣␣␣s

by Kay Cloud

Early 20th cen-
tury sock doll.

by Kay Cloud
Photographs by Ray Cloud

Dedication
To Laura Holtorf Collins and the memory of my mother, Ruby Ardelis Barlow Pulliam.

"Ever she sought the best, ever she found it."
Bettyanne Bethea Twigg

Printed in the United States of America

ISBN: 0-87588-354-0

Published by Hobby House Press
Cumberland,
Maryland 21502

Acknowledgements:

My publisher for his visions, my husband for his hard work and support, the Caldwell Family, Sue Pratt and Silver Dollar City, Rita Williams, Master weaver, each and every customer who has dropped off antique supplies and all the "Wicks, Willits and Twiggs" of the world.

Table of Contents

Foreword 2
General Assembly Instructions 4
Tools and Supplies 6
Body Patterns 7
About Faces 12
Handwork and Finishing 21
Dresses 24
Hats 31

Foreword

The time was when the East was moving West, homesteaders were building frame houses where the log home once stood and life was quiet, simple and humble. Improvising was a daily duty with many rural mothers. They either had the natural ability to "make do" or they had to acquire that ability to survive. Everything was necessary for something and everything was used for something. Every so often a bit of the useful was stashed away for very special gifts — handmade gifts. Grandfathers whittled from wood toys of all sorts and once in awhile they whittled arms and legs for that doll that Mother was about to finish from her deft fingers.

Sawdust, straw and bran were used to stuff the bodies. Bits of various fabrics (Mom always called it material) were used to dress the dolls. Buttons were needed for their own clothes, and therefore seldom used on the dolls. Most of the clothes were sewn directly on the doll body. Stitches ever so small were made with silk thread and ever so tiny needles. It was indeed an art most of us modern day ladies never seem to master.

Faces were that of ladies rather than babies. Some were embroidered, some were penciled and some were painted with homemade paint or vegetable dyes. Many cheeks were rouged with Mother's rouge.

More often than not the caption of the homemade doll will read, "This rag doll is to unknown origin, probably 19th century and is clad in her original dress of homespun linen trimmed with lace, cotton pantalettes and wearing black kid shoes, Where or by whom she was made we shall never know." Dolls of the prairie were not signed or dated by the maker. Clothing and style are the only means of dating.

I believe we are about to see American cloth-bodied dolls come into the spotlight and justly so. Their place in the doll world has been too silent for too long. So simple they are and yet so complexly were some of them styled. Early American mothers were proud to see their dolls setting next to the very store-bought dolls they were trying to emulate.

Small bits and pieces of cloth, special pieces, were saved to dress the doll that some lucky girl or boy would get for that special occasion. The stuffing depended on whatever was abundant and not necessary for the everyday life of the prairie. That could have been sawdust, straw or bran and occasionally newspaper or wadded paper and cotton and wool. Rags were not used abundantly until later in the century. Rags were kept and used for mending and patching wearable clothing. In the early part of the century only the affluent had plenty of rags.

When I was small on the farm in southern Illinois, we made our dolls from clay of the earth or tied rags (we had plenty of rags!) around sticks, or we rolled rags and tied them off at the joints with more rags. I remember only four "store-bought" dolls in my youth. I also do not remember missing "store-bought" dolls. We always knew we could make a doll.

Have you noticed most of our old family photographs were taken in or around the family home? The subjects stood tall and straight, without the faintest of a smile. The early "homemade" dolls depict the same stern face. It was considered flirtatious for ladies to smile in public and they probably did not smile too much at home. It just was not the proper thing to do. If you look closely at old photographs you can easily see the faces and attire of the dolls in them. The dolls were mostly made in the likeness of the mothers. The simple wonderful clothing, like the faces, was also humble and stern. The colors were subtle and plain with the exception of a soft print added in now and then.

Once you have completed your first doll you will easily get the feel of what it was then to make a doll without the assistance of your local hobby shop. It takes some thinking and picking to put the "right" clothes on the right doll. The colors are very important to make the doll seem authentic. Pastels were not available yet and silks and satins were not too plentiful in the Plains states. The use of plain muslin and old sheeting or pillow tubing was a commonly used fabric. Formerly the sheets and pillow slips were purchased from the local mercantile by the yard and then transformed into bedding at the home, by machine if one was owned, if not, they were made by hand. The sewing machine was first introduced in 1849 and by 1859 many

mothers had one. I sew much of my dolls on an 1902 White treadle machine. As a young girl, I learned to sew on a treadle. My mother sewed many flour sack dresses for us girls on that machine.

No makers marks have they, nor do they walk, talk or cry and their eyes remain still, but the elegance of their simplicity will steal your heart and captivate your attention for a lifetime. The hidden history of the American handmade dolls of the 1800s will always cause wonder of where, when and how it began and whose heart it kept at bay during its time. The stories of the handmade dolls goes on and on and on and its history tags always along. I love them, their curiosity, their tattered stained faces and ragged sleeved dresses. I should like to do honor to their creators. I should also hope this will inspire new creators of American history. Perhaps in our up and coming space age, we too, will be wondered about one day. Books teach and inspire, our work does both, I hope I have done that for you.

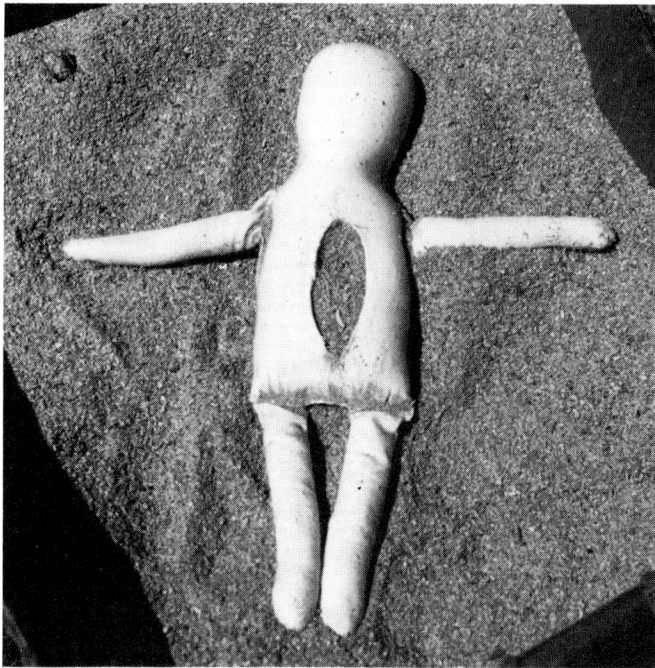

Illustration 1. The back opening for stuffing, and the nearly completed five piece body.

Illustration 2. Tying and stitching procedure for the smaller dolls.

General Assembly Instructions

You are about to undertake and experience a piece of your American heritage. Although we do not have the silk threads and minute needles, we can accomplish the same results and appreciate the talents of our ancestors, the pioneer mothers.

You will need to find a source of good clean sawdust and preferably a coarser grade. The powdery dust can be used, but will require some expertise in packing and stuffing in order to keep the doll firm. Sift all sawdust. I use a kitchen colander. You may want to use a face mask as the sawdust can be tough on the nose! Any type sawdust is acecptable. Naturally, cedar is nice but you may not have access to it.

Trace or transfer your pattern to the unbleached muslin or feed sack. Cut out the pattern pieces. Sew all pieces together, clipping all turns and curves. Be careful not to clip too close or the seam will pull out while stuffing. If you are going to use my exact face pattern, you will need to use a transfer pen and proceed with that step before you sew the body pieces together. It can be done after, but with some difficulty.

Most any problem you have can be solved and worked around if you just think about it. Remember, you do not have to be perfect. Isn't that a relief!

Assembly For The Two Piece Body

Cut out, sew around entire body, clip all curves and turns. Make the slit in the back and turn body through the slit. (See *Illustration 1*.) Stuff the arms and legs; tie off at shoulders and hips. Stuff the head and body, leaving enough room at the slit to sew together. (*Illustration 2*.) Tie off at the neck and the doll is ready to tea stain. I spray the tea on and allow to dry overnight. On a sunny day it would easily dry in a couple of hours. Once she is dry, she is ready to dress.

Assembly For The Five Piece Body

Cut, sew, clip and turn all pieces. (*Illustration 3*.) Stuff the arms and legs. Fold under 1/4in (.65cm) to 1/2in (1cm) of body bottom at the arm and leg placement. (*Illustration 4*.) Sew on arms and legs. Make a slit in the back and stuff the head and body. Stuff the neck area tightly. Also stuff the entire body and parts tightly for a long life. The face can be painted or embroidered now along with the hair. I always embroider after the doll is stuffed, leaving my knots in the hairline. If you choose to embroider before stuffing, you may find the facial features will change dramatically after stuffing. Sometimes I find my faces change dramatically regardless of what I do! After the face of your choice, tea dye. Dry and dress.

About Tea Dying

If you tea dye the "material" before you make the clothes and dry them, you will get an even color of aging. If you make the clothes, dress the doll and then spray her with tea, you will get more aging on the folds.

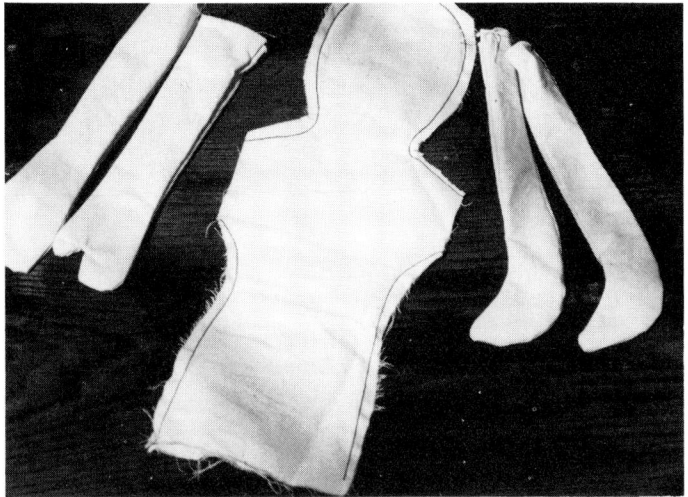

Illustration 3. Five piece body parts ready for stuffing and assembly.

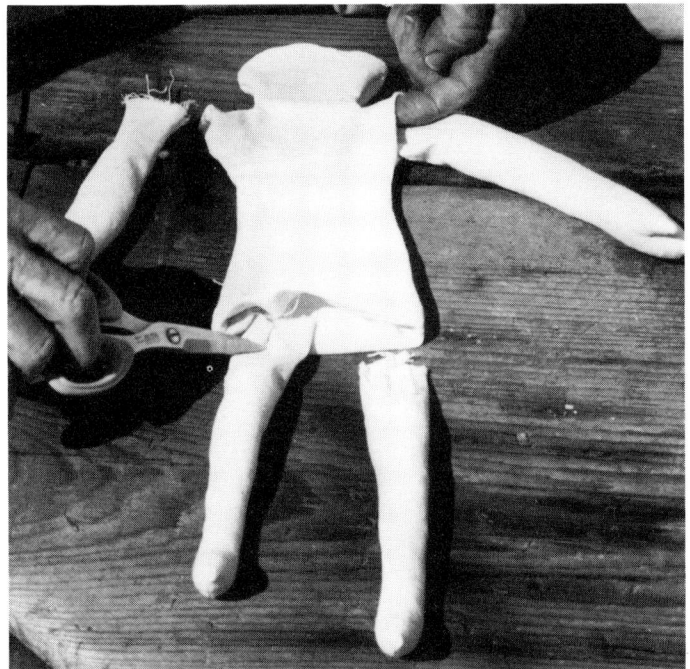

Illustration 4. Fold under 1/4" to 1/2" of bottom of body before attaching the legs.

Supplies And Tools Needed

Sawdust (about a 3lb. coffee can full)
Embroidery needle and thread
Sewing scissors
Long-handled wooden spoon (for stuffing)
Instant tea (1 cup)
Acrylic or oil paints
Wool yarn
Unbleached muslin 1yd (91cm) or one feed
    sack
Print dress scraps 1/2yd (46cm)
Plain muslin 1/4yd (23cm)
Tracing paper or pen

1 flat paint brush
1 liner paint brush
Antique handkerchiefs, 2 or 3
ALL OF THE SEAMS TAKEN ARE 1/4in
    (0.65cm)

Instant Tea Recipe
1 cup instant tea to 1½ gallons hot water

Noteworthy

Since we all stuff differently, you may have to make minor adjustments to clothing or you can lay the doll on the fabric and cut her dress around her. That would be the way the pioneer mothers would have done it. They did not have patterns. Be real; think pioneer!

Some of the simple household tools used in making sawdust dolls.

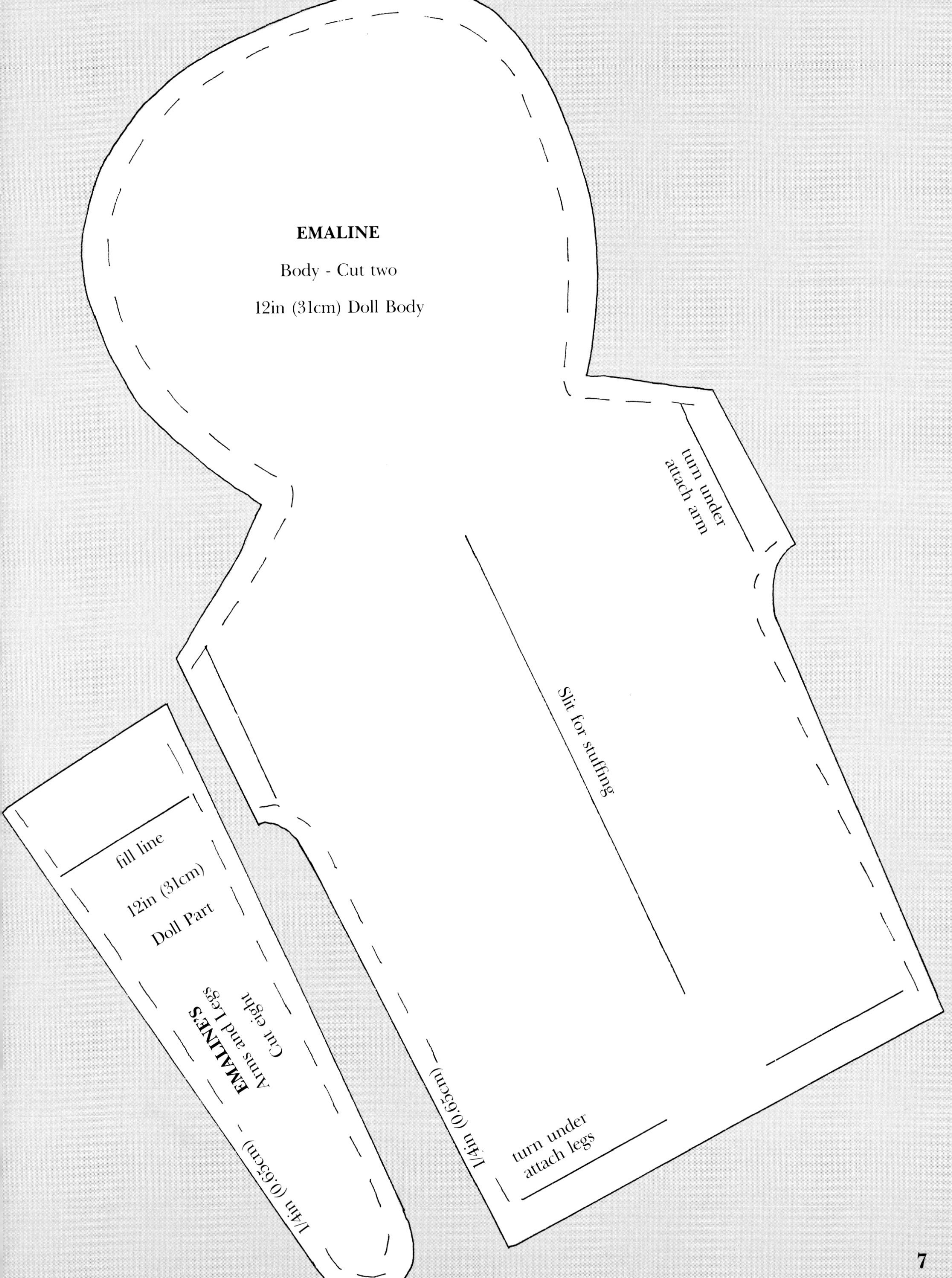

EMALINE

Body - Cut two

12in (31cm) Doll Body

turn under
attach arm

Slit for stuffing

fill line

12in (31cm)

Doll Part

EMALINE'S
Arms and Legs
Cut eight

1/4in (0.65cm)

1/4in (0.65cm)

turn under
attach legs

7

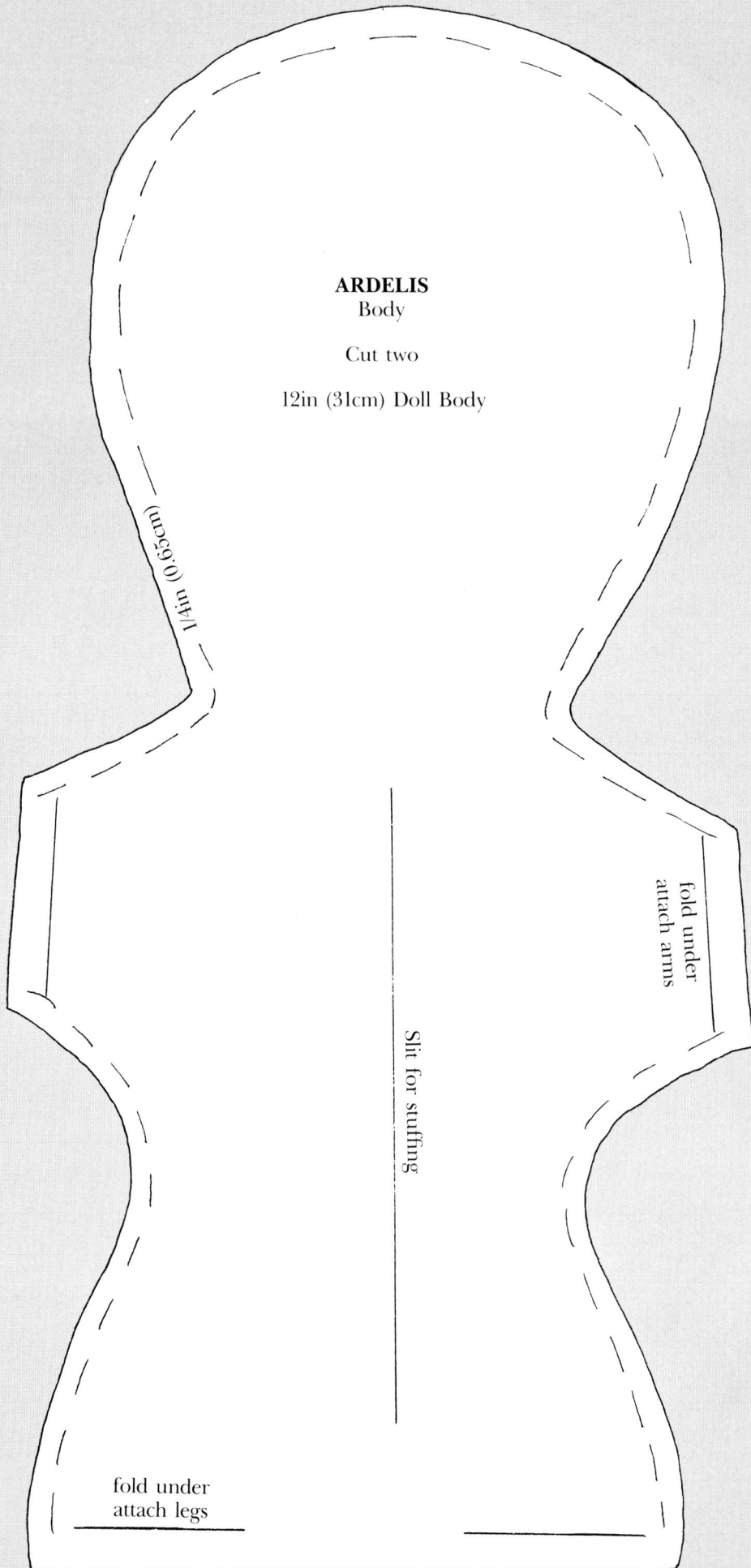

ARDELIS
Body

Cut two

12in (31cm) Doll Body

1/4in (0.635cm)

Slit for stuffing

fold under
attach arms

fold under
attach legs

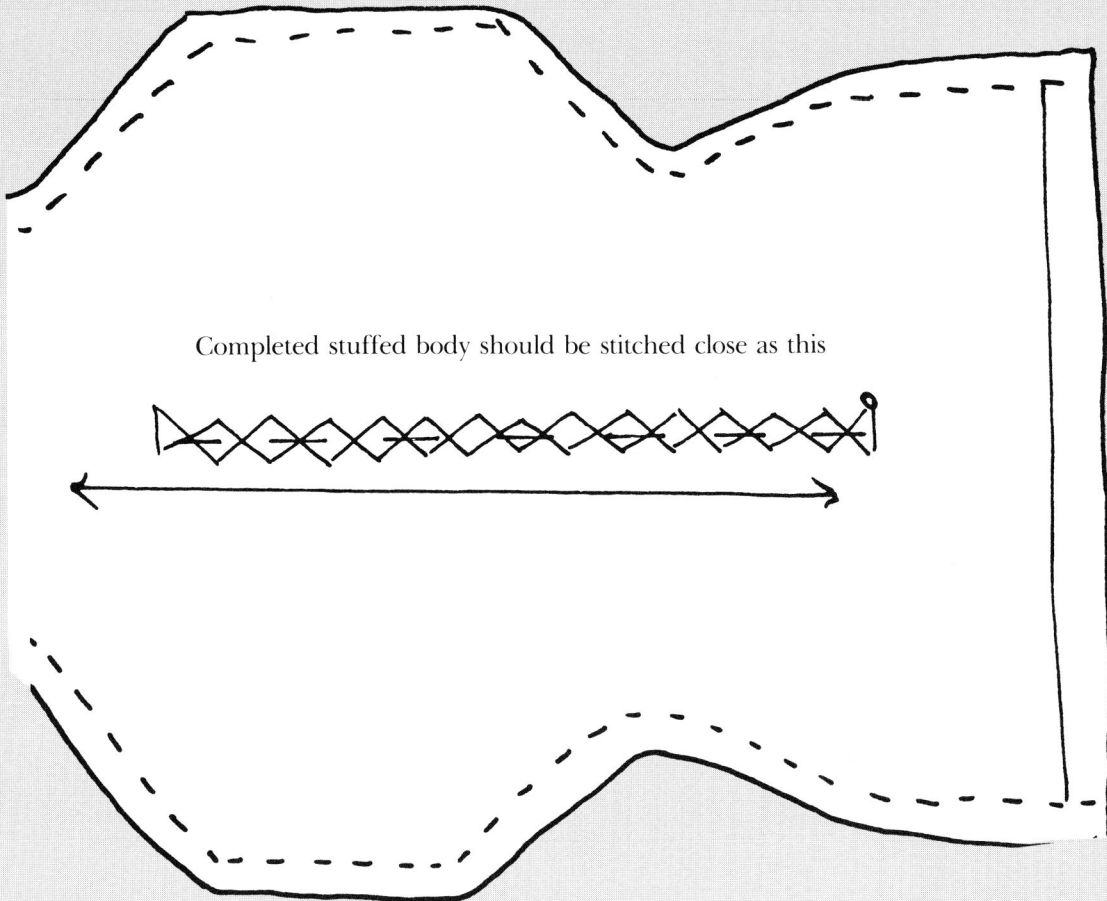

Completed stuffed body should be stitched close as this

Illustration of sewing on the back after the doll has been stuffed.

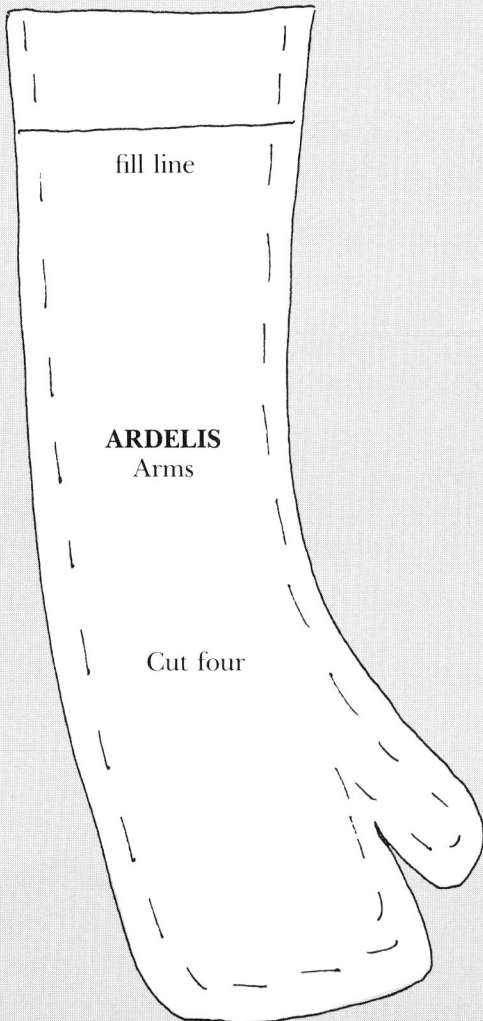

fill line

ARDELIS
Arms

Cut four

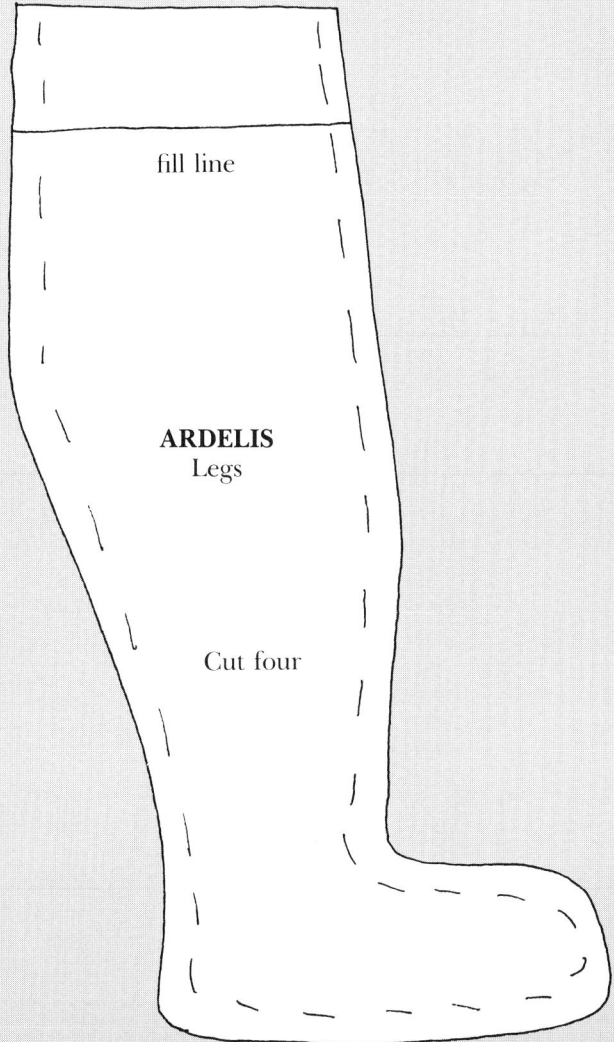

fill line

ARDELIS
Legs

Cut four

ELLIE

10in (25cm) Doll

Cut two

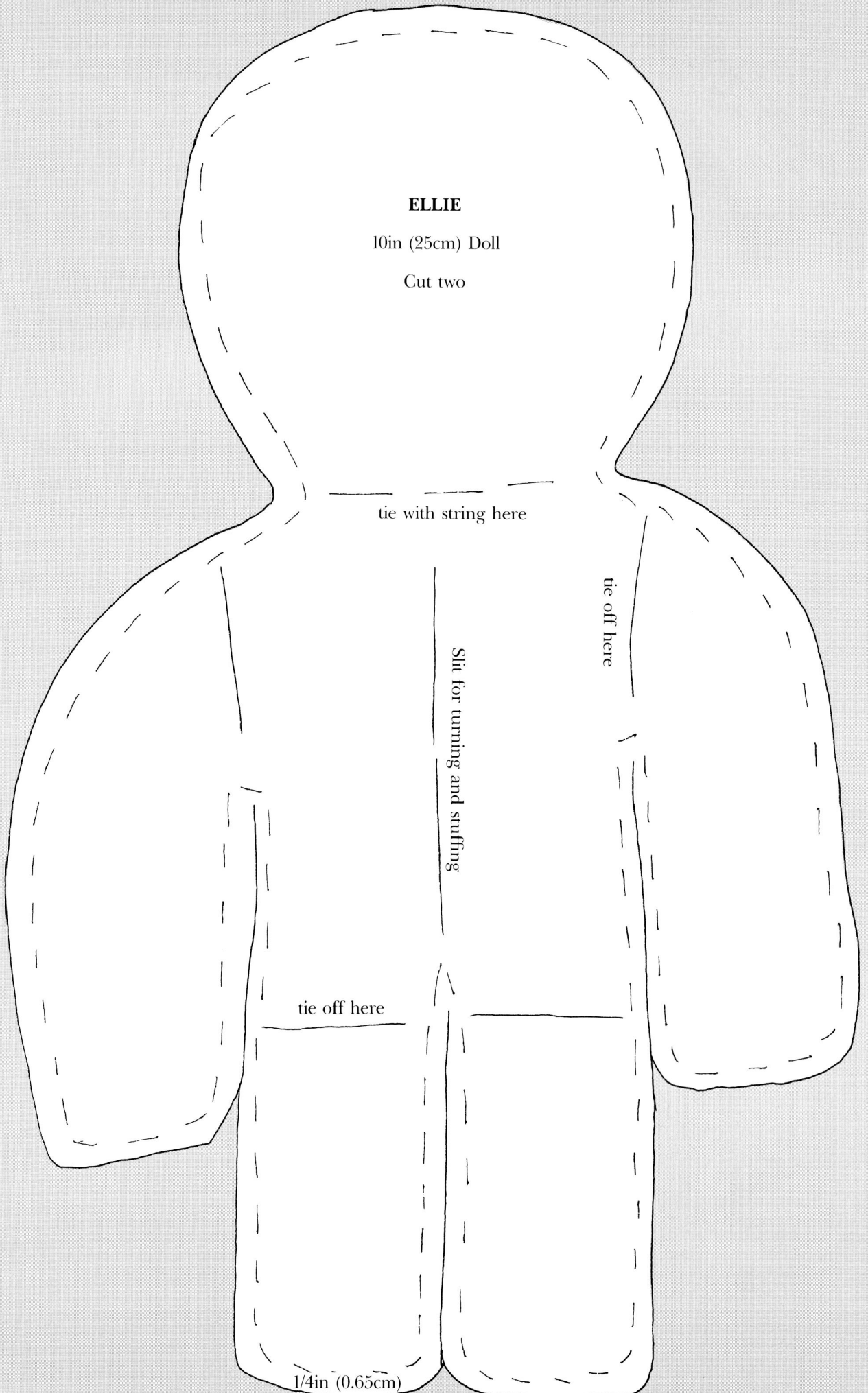

tie with string here

tie off here

Slit for turning and stuffing

tie off here

1/4in (0.65cm)

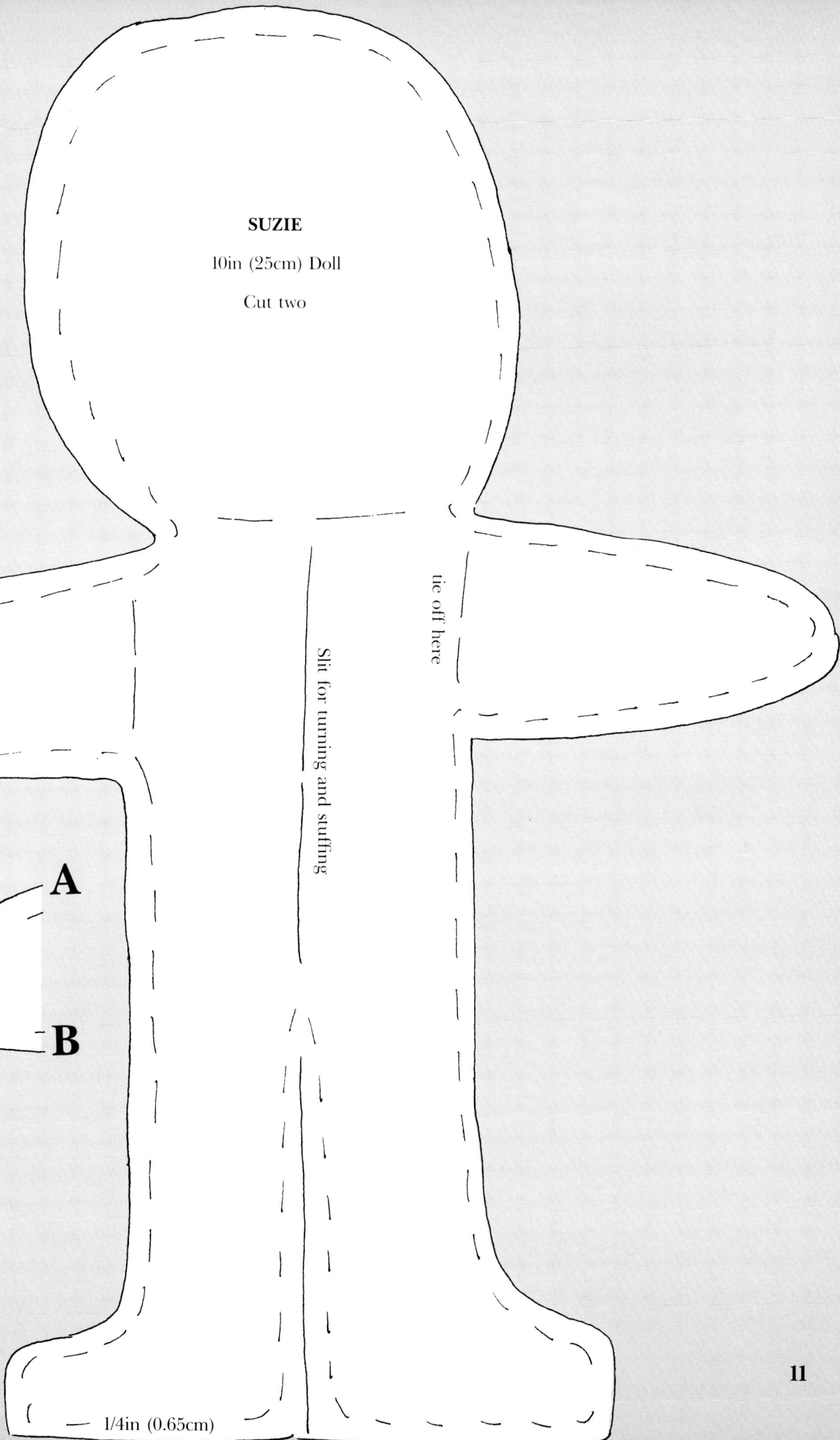

SUZIE

10in (25cm) Doll

Cut two

A

B

tie off here

Slit for turning and stuffing

A

B

1/4in (0.65cm)

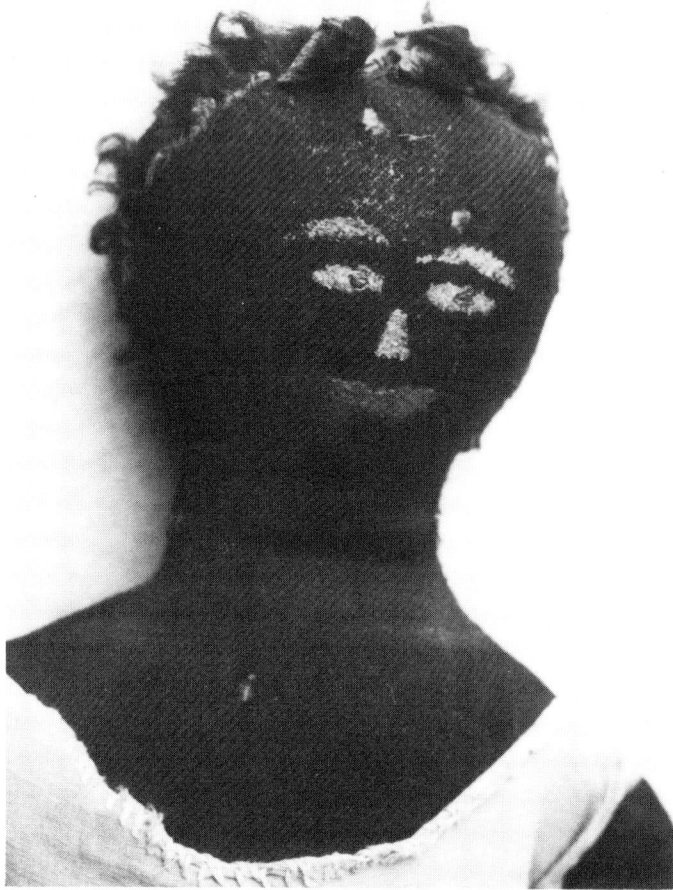

Dinah has a wool gabardine body filled with various scraps of wool yarn. She was created by Grammie Dawes for Hope Coffin in Auburn, Maine. *Frances Marsh Collection, Gorham, Maine.*

About Faces

The greatest part of making early American-type dolls is the fact that you do not have to be an artist to do the faces. Pioneer mothers were not artists. They were simply making a plaything for a child. Simple. Try to make exactly the same face as the pattern and you will surely be disappointed. Use the pattern as a guideline and you will find the face and doll belongs to you. For those of you who want a face you can live with, I strongly suggest *Another Pretty Face* by Elspeth published by Hobby House Press, Inc. It is truly a big help and many of my customers are thoroughly pleased with it.

Faces - Embroidered

Materials needed:

1 skein each brown, black and rose embroidery floss
1/4 pound of handspun wool or 1 skein of dark yarn, brown or black

Instructions:

Pencil or transfer by graphite paper the pattern to the stuffed doll. If you choose to embroider the face before you stuff the doll, you will find the features will change. I suggest embroidery after stuffing. Use a long embroidery needle or tapestry needle. Keeping the knots in the edge of the hair line or side head seams while you embroider, when the face is complete you can clip the knots out of the side head seam. Use simple stitches. I call it the minute stitch with a satin stitch for the pupils of the eyes. Do not forget the ears. To attach the yarn, just use regular thread, brown or black, and throw the thread over the yarn or wool.

Completed dolls from given patterns in this book.

20th century sawdust dolls in various styles from history.

Sawdust doll with soft head and painted features.

Sawdust doll with varnished head and stitched nose.

20th century sawdust dolls.

Sawdust doll with embroidered face and wool yarn hair.

18

Author demonstrating stuffing bodies at the first DOLL READER-SILVER DOLLAR CITY DOLL CHALLENGE Show and Sale.

Painted Faces

Materials needed:

Acrylics or oils — brown, black, red iron io-
   xide, antique white, and rose.
#2 flat brush
#8 flat brush
#0 or #1 liner brush

Instructions:

Keep your brush reasonably dry, i.e.,
dip it in the cleaner (water for acrylics and
turpentine for oils), blot all of the liquid out
and then blot again. Do the eyebrows first,
nose and eyes last. Put in the mouth. Make
a little shading around the eyes with a very
dry brush. **Always**, after putting your brush
in the paint, make one stroke on your pallet
to soften the amount of paint on the brush.
Test the paint on the brush before putting
it on the face. The drier you keep the
brush, the softer your face will be. Blush
the cheeks with a strictly dry brush and
keep a gentle touch. You can always darken
any feature once you have it in place, but it
is sometimes difficult to take away extra
paint.

It would be good to practice on a piece
of fabric before you start the face just to get
the feel of how the paint is going to be ap-
plied on fabric. I would not use fabric me-
dium. It is not necessary. The paint will not
wash or wear off. Just get it on your clothes
and you will be a believer! Once oil and
acrylics have dried, they are permanent.

Hair:

You will need to use a wetter brush for
the hair. The floating technique has a good
effect on hair. Keep the darker color next
to the face.

Illustration 5. 20th century sawdust doll with painted hair, sawdust filled, charcoal facial features with pokeberry dye on the cheeks.

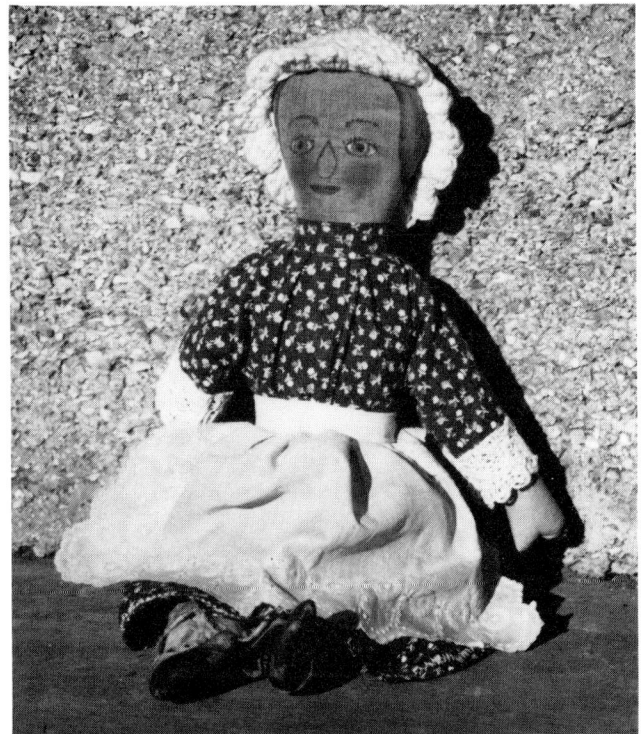

Illustration 6. 20th century sawdust doll, soft face and head with painted features.

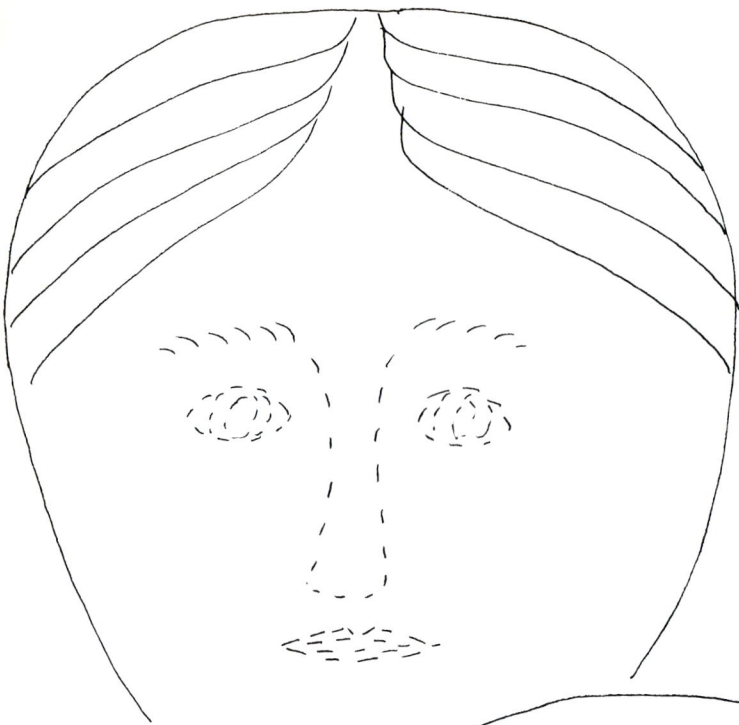

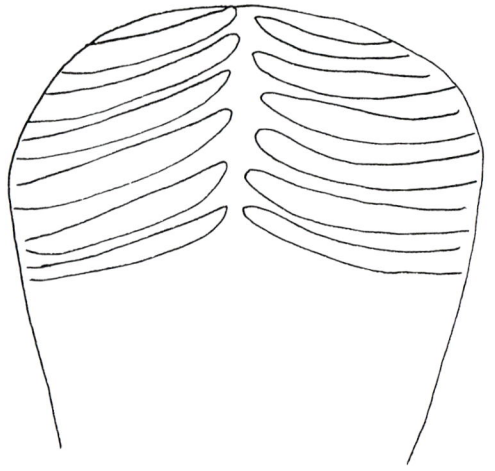

ABOVE:
Stitched face with yarn hair.

Painted faces.

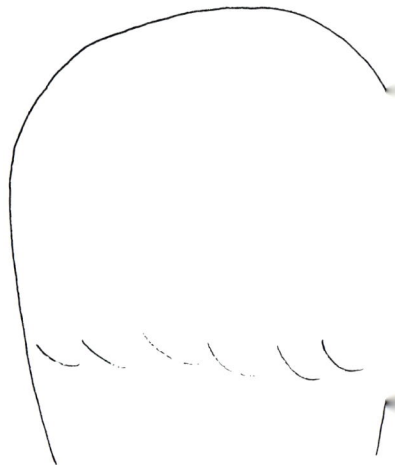

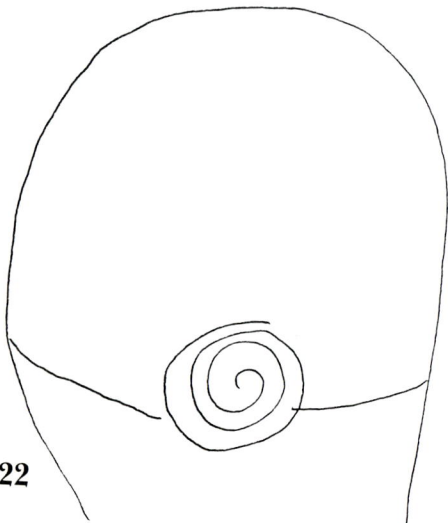

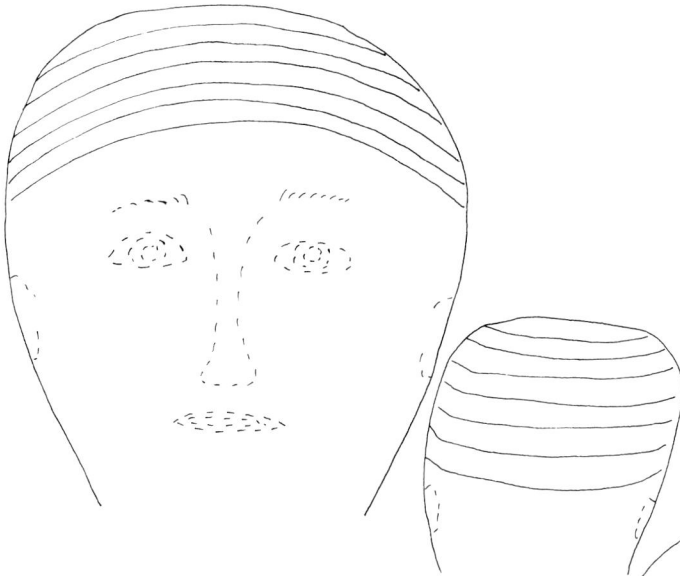

The yard is handspun wool and is whipstitched on the stuffed doll head.

Painted faces are rather simple but some knowledge of painting is required.

Illustration 7. Handspun wool yarn is braided and stitched on a soft head by simply throwing the thread over the yarn and sewing to the head. A single strand of yarn can be used in the same manner as pictured on the right.

Illustration 8. Left photo shows painted head, right photo shows stitched wool yarn hair.

Dressing The 12in (31cm) Doll

Materials needed:
Pantaloons
1/4yd (23cm) soft cotton
8in (20cm) lace or trim
Slip
1/4yd (23cm) cotton
12in (31cm) lace or trim
A piece of cotton fabric 1/4yd (23cm) by 36in (91cm) will make both the pantaloons and slip.

Slip assembly:
Cut out the garment pieces and using a 1/4in (0.65cm) seam, sew the shoulder pieces together. Turn under 1/4in (0.65cm) at armholes and hem. Starting at the armholes, sew the side seams taking a 1/4in (0.65cm) seam allowance. Finish by either taking 1/2in (1cm) hem or turn under the same allowance and add lace or trim.

Pantaloon assembly:
Cut out the pieces and taking 1/4in (0.65cm) seam allowance, sew together at the shoulders. Taking the same seam allowance turn fabric under 1/4in (0.65cm) and hem the armholes. You should also add your lace or trim to the armholes now. With the same seam allowance, starting at the armhole, sew the side seams as well as the center seams. Hem using 1/2in (1cm) seam allowance. The lace or trim can be added by machine or hand at the leg openings. First place the pantaloons on the doll. Using a quilters thread run, or by hand a gather stitch, and turning under the raw edges as you proceed, gather to fit the doll's neck and secure by tying off.

Placing the slip on the doll, complete the neck in the same fashion, turning under 1/4in (0.65cm) raw edges as you gather to complete the slip.

Dress A For The 12in (31cm) Doll

Materials needed:
3/8yd (0.33cm) calico or print cotton
1yd (91cm) lace or trim

Cut out dress pieces. With right sides together, using 1/4in (0.65cm) seam allowances, sew the shoulder seams. Gather the sleeves where indicated; this can be done by hand or machine. Using a 1/4in (0.65cm) seam, sew the gathered sleeve onto the bodice. Add the trim or lace to the sleeve edge, turning under the 1/4in (0.65cm) allowance as you sew the trim on. With the sleeves sewn in place, hemmed and trimmed, starting at the sleeve edge, right sides together, sew the side seams using the same seam allowance of 1/4in (0.65cm). Lay the bodice flat on a table. Starting from the bottom of the bodice in the center of what will be the dress back, cut the back opening completely to the neck opening. The center back of the dress skirt will match up to the center back bodice opening you have just made.

Using the same seam allowance, sew with right sides together the side seams of the skirt. Lay skirt flat on a table, find the center and from the waist make a 3in (8cm) opening in the skirt. Starting 1/8in (0.31cm) at the waist of the skirt, gather to fit the bodice. Sew, taking a 1/4in (0.65cm) seam, the skirt to the bodice, matching to the back openings. Cut the neckband to fit your doll's neck, fold in half, sew in the neckhole keeping the raw edges to the wrong side of the neckhole with a 1/4in (0.65cm) seam. Hem with a 1/2in (1cm) fold at the bottom of the dress. If you choose to add lace to the hemline do so after hemming.

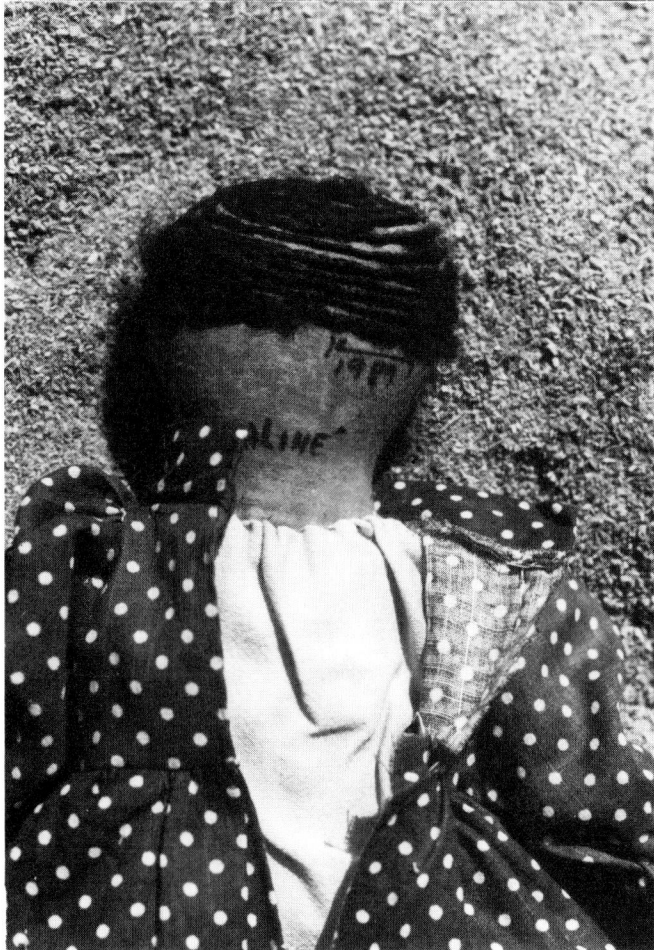

Illustration 9. Note stitching at neck of underslip.

Illustration 10. Hand stitch the back opening of the dress and fine tune the doll.

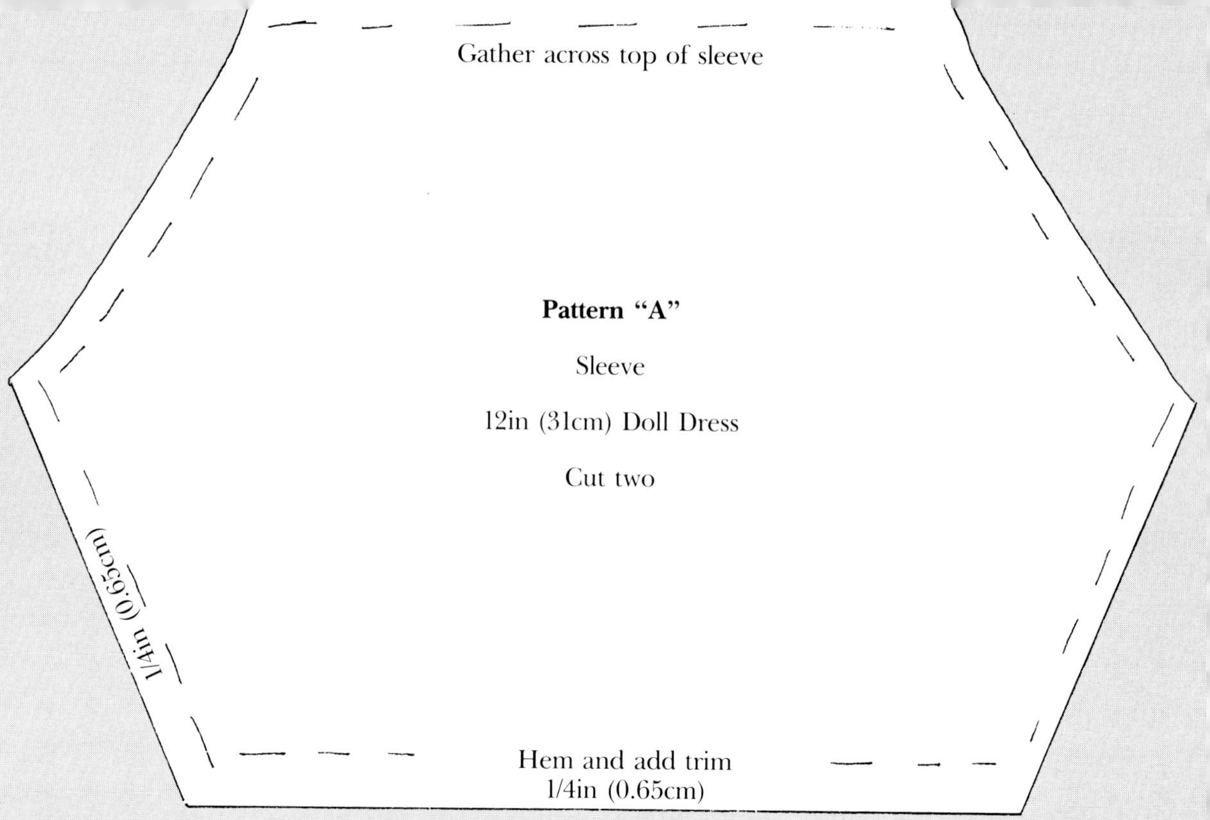

Gather across top of sleeve

Pattern "A"

Sleeve

12in (31cm) Doll Dress

Cut two

1/4in (0.65cm)

Hem and add trim
1/4in (0.65cm)

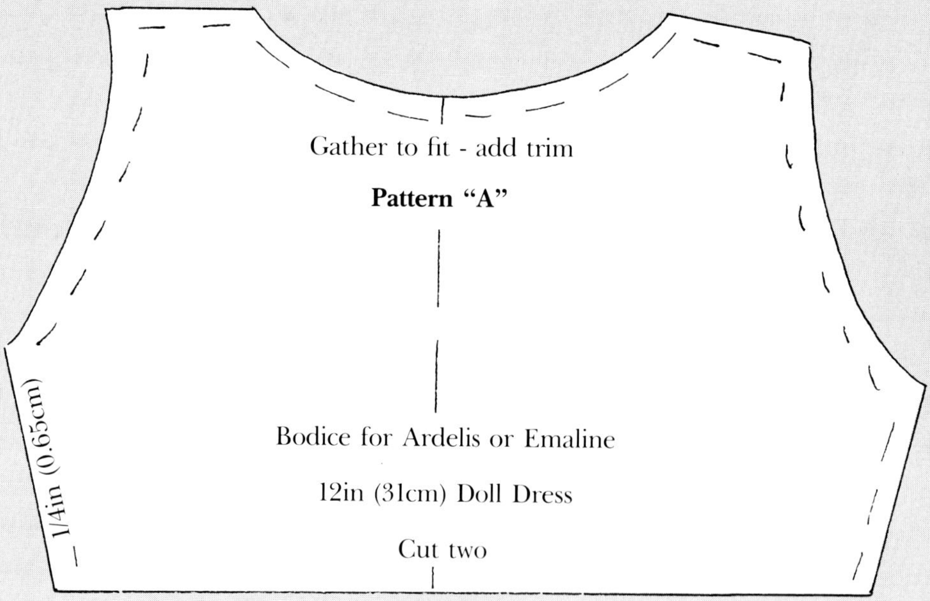

Gather to fit - add trim

Pattern "A"

Bodice for Ardelis or Emaline

12in (31cm) Doll Dress

Cut two

1/4in (0.65cm)

1/4in (0.65cm)

Pattern "A"

Neckband

Cut one

12in (31cm) Doll Dress

Center fold here

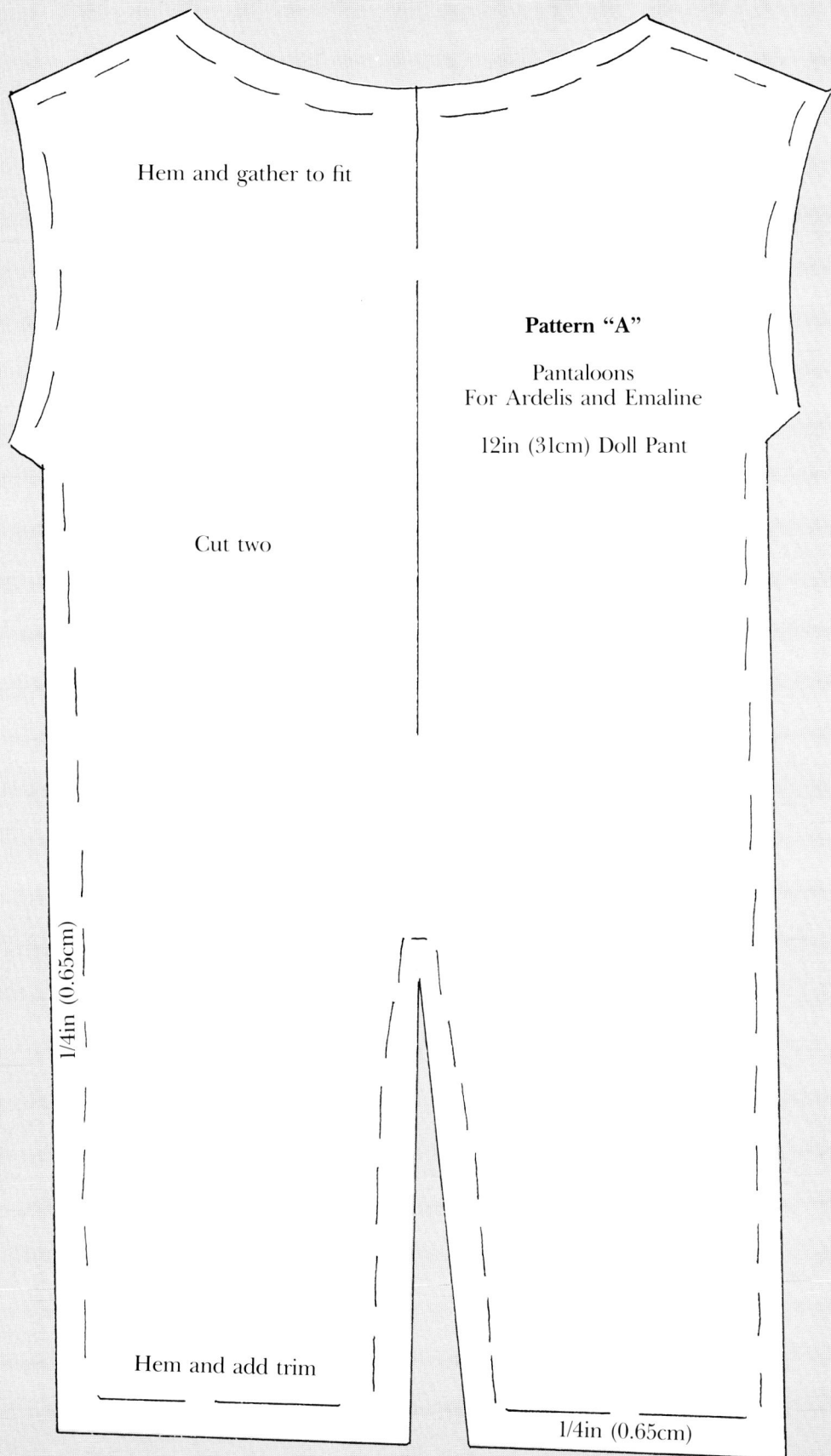

Hem and gather to fit

Pattern "A"

Pantaloons
For Ardelis and Emaline

12in (31cm) Doll Pant

Cut two

1/4in (0.65cm)

Hem and add trim

1/4in (0.65cm)

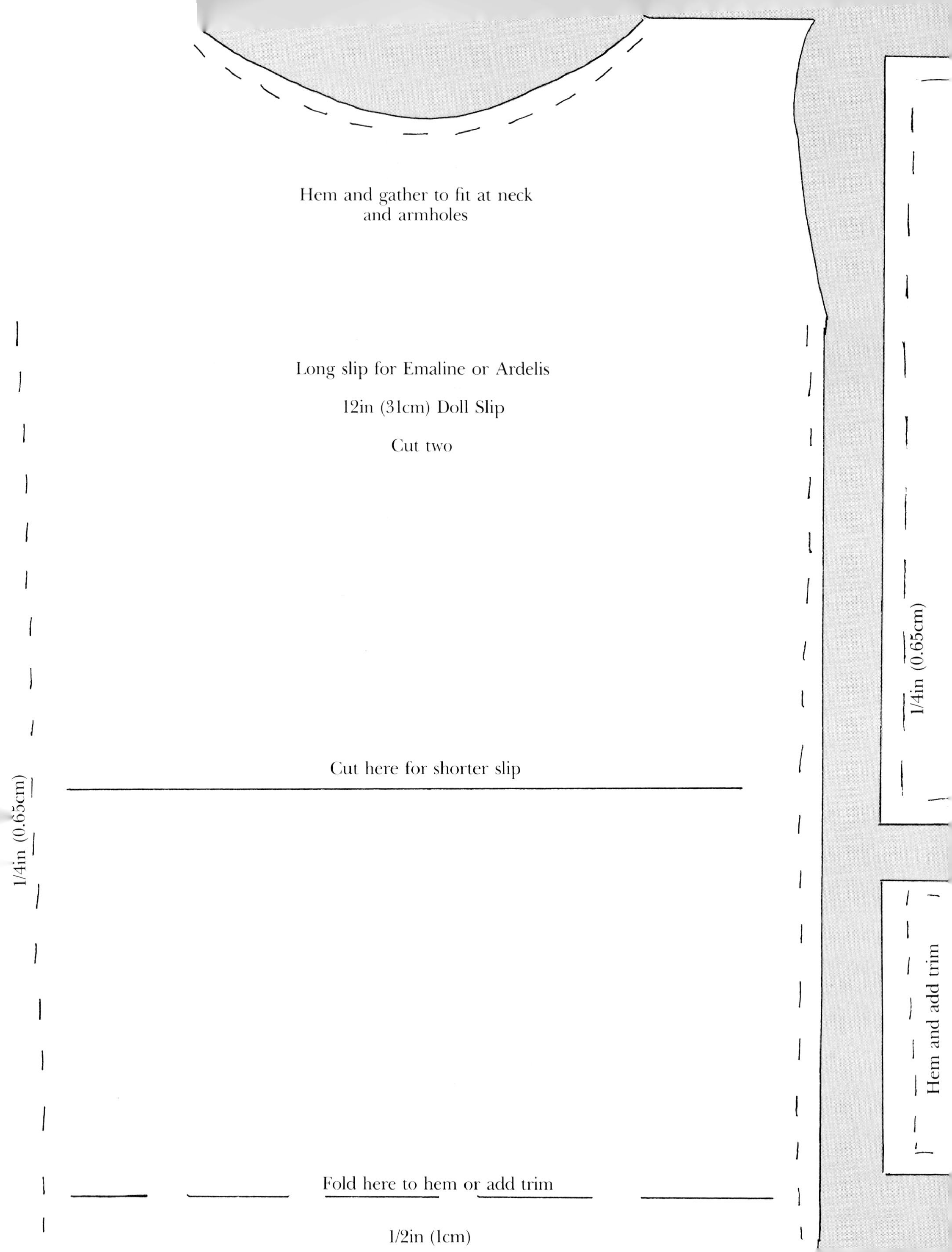

Hem and gather to fit at neck
and armholes

Long slip for Emaline or Ardelis

12in (31cm) Doll Slip

Cut two

Cut here for shorter slip

1/4in (0.65cm)

1/4in (0.65cm)

1/4in (0.65cm)

Hem and add trim

Fold here to hem or add trim

1/2in (1cm)

Gather to fit

Dress Skirt for 12in (31cm) Doll

Cut two

FOLD

Hem and add lace

1/4in (0.65cm)

1/4in (0.65cm)

Add neckband

Dress Bodice for 12in (31cm) Doll

Cut two

FOLD

Dress "B" For 12in (31cm) Doll

Materials required:

1/4yd (23m) cotton print

1yd (91m) lace or trim

Assembly:

Cut out two dress pieces on the fold. With right sides together, sew the shoulder/ sleeve seam using 1/4in (0.65cm) seam allowance. Using the same seam allowance, hem the sleeves and add the lace or trim now. Using the same seam allowance, sew the side seams. Add the lace or trim to the dress bottom now. You can add as you hem by turning under the hem, pressing in place, placing the lace on the right side of the dress hem and sew in place. The dress will be hemmed too. For a shorter or smock type dress, cut the pattern off at the first pattern length mark. For a longer dress, use the entire pattern, or if you want a very long dress, add length to the pattern. You can machine gather the neckline or hand gather using the same 1/4in (0.65cm) allowance. If you are hand gathering the neckline, place the dress on the doll, turn under the seam allowance as you sew, gathering at the same time. Allow yourself about 10in (25cm) extra on the string or thread you are gathering with, allowing you to tie a bow with the gather thread. You can use the neckband from Dress "A" pattern also. Cut the neckband to fit your doll's neck. Make an opening 3in (8cm) down the center back of the dress, starting at the neckline. Sew the neckband in place using a 1/4in (0.65cm) seam. Dress the doll and hand secure the back neck opening.

Fold

1/4in (0.65cm)

Slip for 10in (25cm) Doll

Gather to fit waist

1/4in (0.65cm)

Hem or add trim here

allow 1/4in (0.65cm) for hem
or lace attachment

1/4in (0.65cm)

Gather to fit and add trim

FOLD

Pattern "B"

Dress for
Emaline or Ardelis

12in (31cm) Doll Dress

Cut two

Cut here for shorter dress

Allow 1/2in (1cm) for hem

Hem or add trim
allow 1/2in (1cm) for hem

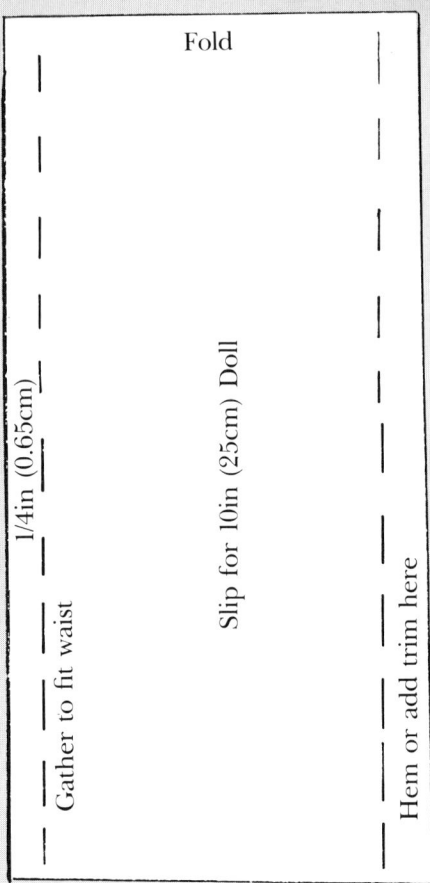

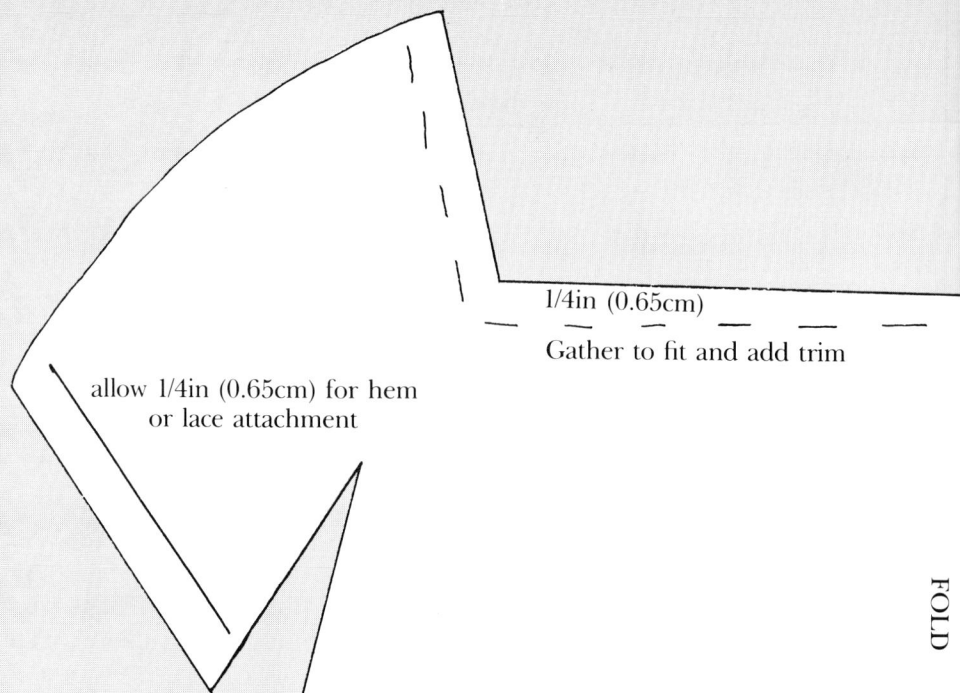

Antique Handkerchief Dresses For Ellie Or Suzie

When choosing your handkerchief, make sure it has lots of handwork or lacey edging. They are usually trimmed on all sides; therefore, all you have to do is stitch two-thirds the way up each side, leaving the last third open for the armhole. Trim out the center (see pattern), make a small back slit, gather at the neck to fit your doll, add a neckband of lace or coordinating fabric, slip the dress on the doll and hand sew up the back.

Many hours were spent trimming the handkerchiefs by our ancestors. Although pioneer mothers would not have used them for doll dresses, they did fancy themselves in carrying their fine handwork to church on Sunday. There were "everday" handkerchiefs and "Sunday" handkerchiefs. I can see my grandmother doing handwork on hers. "Everdays" had rather plain trim or none at all, but the "Sundays" were quite elaborate and dainty — as elaborate and dainty as Grandmother herself.

Pantaloons For Ellie Or Suzie

See Pantaloon assembly for Emaline and Ardelis.

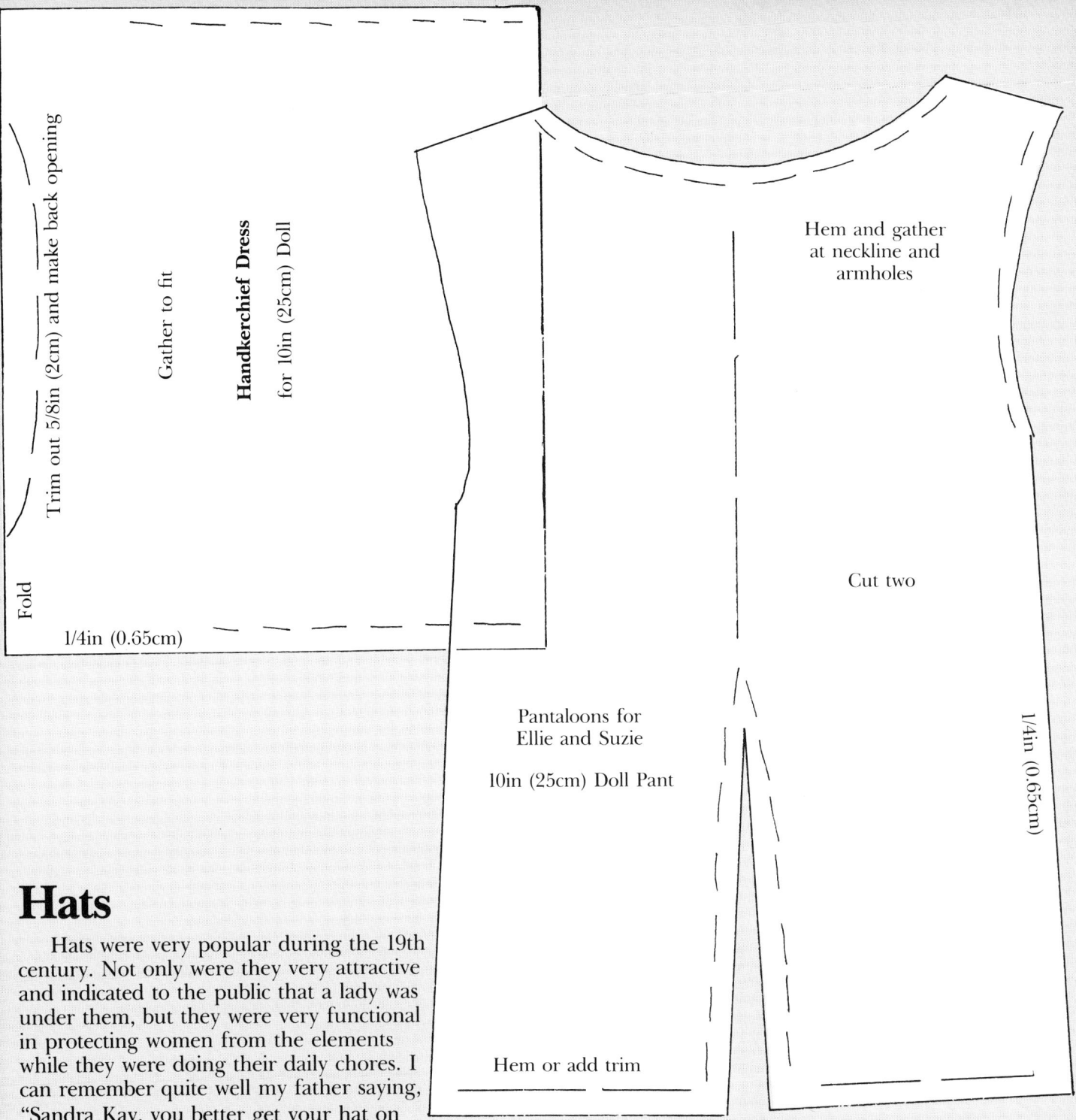

Trim out 5/8in (2cm) and make back opening

Gather to fit

Handkerchief Dress

for 10in (25cm) Doll

Fold

1/4in (0.65cm)

Hem and gather
at neckline and
armholes

Cut two

1/4in (0.65cm)

Pantaloons for
Ellie and Suzie

10in (25cm) Doll Pant

Hem or add trim

Hats

Hats were very popular during the 19th century. Not only were they very attractive and indicated to the public that a lady was under them, but they were very functional in protecting women from the elements while they were doing their daily chores. I can remember quite well my father saying, "Sandra Kay, you better get your hat on or you will get freckles." Well, that was a wasted statement as freckles I have many and hats as well.

Hats seem to change the character of the dolls. When you want to change a "plain" doll to a proper lady, just add a hat.

It only takes a small "rag" to make a hat. You can gather a square piece of "material" on three sides and have a charming hat. Tie off at the neck. Dig into the "rag bag" and come up with some new creations of your own.

Years ago when mothers were obliged to exercise their taste with much fewer luxuries, the fabrics were simple. A "rag bag" was found in every home, frequently sorted through when a special piece was needed. Mob caps, floppy hats and bonnets were most popular and functional. Some of the larger brims were laced with strips of "cardboard" to keep the shape. They were inserted so they could be removed when washed — on Mondays, of course!

Shawls and Capes

Shawls can easily be made by taking your favorite knitted or crocheted doily that might not be suitable for use and cutting it in half, whip in a hem and tie on the doll. Capes can be made in the same way using ruffles and pleated ruffles from old dresses and skirts. Cut a strip off about three times the doll's neck and shoulder area, gather at the neck and hem. Sew on ties and you have a cape. Gathering a straight piece of fabric will give you the same garment. Make the cape long enough to hang at least below the doll's waist.

Rag Hat

Fits all patterns in this book

Materials needed:

8in (20cm) square piece of heavy cotton (drapery weight)
   (For floppy hat use softer cotton.)

Assembly of the rag hat

With right sides together, using a 1/4in (0.65cm) seam allowance, sew two pieces together. Turn and press flat. Using 1/4in (0.65cm) seam allowance, gather the third oval to fit the brim. Stitch to the brim. Add fancies to the hat if you desire.

Shoes

Materials required:

Black or brown paint - oils or acrylics whichever you are using for the rest of the dolls painted features
28in (71cm) of buttonhole thread or string for ties - use half for each shoe

Instructions:

Paint the shoe on as shown in *Illustration 11*. Allow the paint to dry and sew your strings onto the shoes as indicated in *Illustrations 12* and *13*. Tie the laces at the top of the shoe when you are finished stitching the laces, cut off any excess shoe string. Completed shoe will resemble *Illustration 14*.

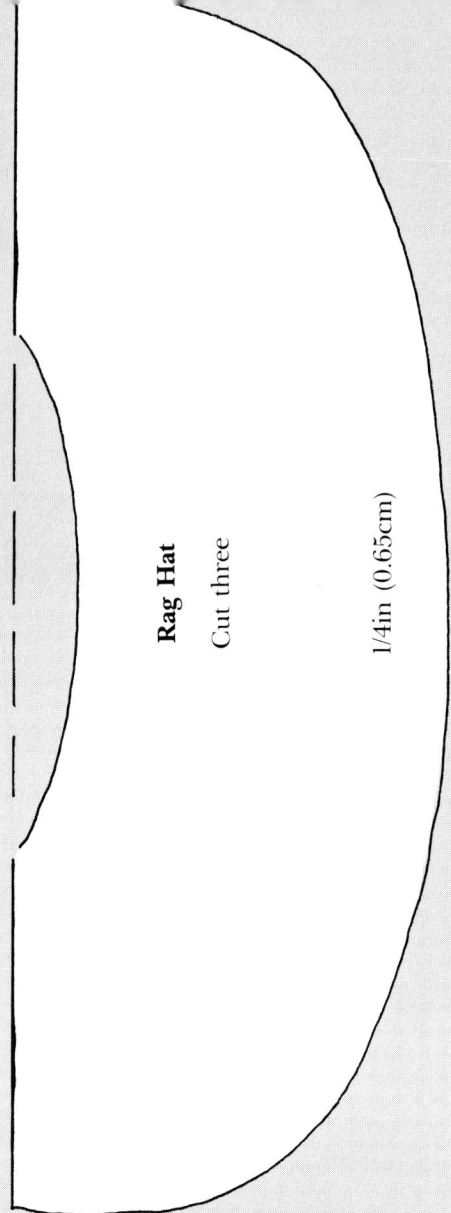

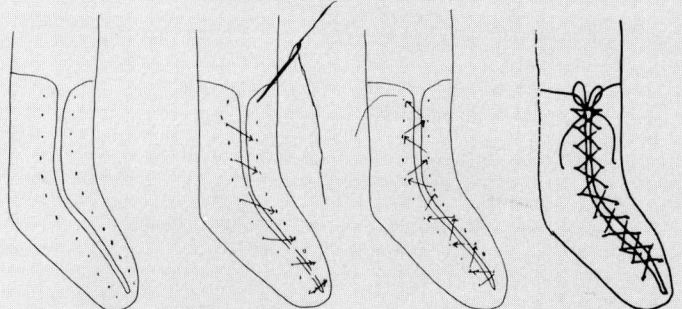

Rag Hat

Cut three

1/4in (0.65cm)

Illustration 11. Illustration 12. Illustration 13. Illustration 14.